The Secret
And the
Truth
Of the
Ages

By
Mark Cordova

Outskirts Press, Inc.
http://www.outskirtspress.com

ISBN: 978-1-4787-1954-0

www.outskirtspress.com/thesecretandthetruthoftheages
www.thesecretandthetruthoftheages.com

PRINTED IN THE UNITED STATES OF AMERICA

Table of Contents

The Secret and the Truth of the Ages

Introduction

Before you read this book, I warn you, your Inner eye and your Inner ear will be opened. You will become the person who you truly are and not the person who you think you are.

You will understand that everything you have ever been taught by the societies of this world has been false. Few people on this earth have tried, but have never been able to completely understand the complete knowledge of the Truth.

Why are we here? Where did we come from? Where are we going? Questions like these will be answered in this book.

Upon reading this book your first impression will be, how can anyone explain this? Who does this person think he is that he can explain these things? Well, even though this will be your first impression, if you continue reading, you will understand. You see, first thought in this material universe is jealousy…and we will explain why.

The greatest person of all, whose name is, "Holy Man," came here close to 2,000 years ago to explain this truth. But because of the nature of this material universe, two entities have been doing the best that they can to make sure that this truth be not known.

In the Very Beginning
The Father

Before the very beginning can be explained, you must understand that existence existed before the very beginning.

What and/or who is existence? Existence is pure ineffable mind. Existence has always existed. Existence was, is, and will always be. There is no time in existence. Existence is the same person that Christ called, The Father. You see, the Father does not really have a name. All who have a name were given their name by someone who existed before them.

The Father does not only not have a name but is also invisible, for there was no one before him to see him. Because he existed before everything, his quantity and his quality cannot be known. He is limitless, for there was no one before him to set limits upon him. Time does not exist in him. He is timeless. Existence will be explained further, later on in this book.

Now that there is some understanding about existence, of whom Christ calls the Father, the very beginning can now be explained.

The Mother

If something does not make sense, then it is probably not true. Even little children know this without explanation. So let us make sense of this. Think to yourself, if you were the Father, what would be your first thought being that there is only you? His first thought was the opposite of himself. Since he has never been seen and he is invisible, then his opposite would be his image, the image of himself.

Everything that is and everything that is not has an opposite to it. Take, for example, this material universe. It is the opposite of the Eternal Realm. The Eternal Realm is eternal. The material universe is not eternal. Do you see the opposition of the two? Do not get confused. The material universe is not his image. This will also be explained further on in this book.

Getting back to the Father, his first thought was the image of himself. Therefore if he is the Father then his image must be the Mother. His image, or the Mother, is the very beginning or the beginning of everything. It makes sense that a mother is the opposite of a father.

So now, the Mother has a name. It is the first name ever given, and of course it was given to her by the Father. Her name is, believe it or not, MAN. This is the true sacred secret. This is the secret that religion and government never want you to know.

You see, the Son (Christ) is the child of the Father and the Holy Spirit, and the Holy Spirit's name is MAN. And yes, the Holy Spirit is female. What sense does it make that a son comes from two men? A son comes from a father and a mother. You can get a better understanding of this when you look at the scriptures.

Christ never really said that he was the son of god. This one, who called himself, god, made up the word and the meaning of this word called god. Religion did its best to make us believe that Christ said that he was the son of god, through forgery and editing. But you can read and see for yourself.

What did Christ really say then? He said plainly and clearly, "I AM THE SON OF MAN."

The Father does not have a name. The Holy Spirit does. That is why he says this.

The True Trinity

What does he say of the Father? He says that, "the Father within me doeth the work." The same Father that is within him is within you. It is your mind. Your invisible mind is the Father within you, not your brain that is material. And the images that you see in your mind, that is the Holy Spirit within you.

Now, Christ, the Son, is also called, "The Word." What is a word? When I say to you, tree, do you see the letters t, r, e, e in your mind or do you see an image of a tree? Of course, you see an image of a tree. Therefore, the Father is mind or mental, and the Mother is image. So then, the Son or Word is the two in one. The Word within you is a mental image.

You see, the true trinity is not outside of you, but it is within you. Religion and government want you to look outside yourself to a god that doesn't exist anymore. Because the true kingdom of heaven is within you, and is eternal, everything outside your true self, even your body is not eternal. Your body, all material, and this whole material universe, belongs to the first god who is no more. And just like he is no more, so will all of his material universe be as well. But you are not of this world, just like Christ said, "I am not of this world." You are not even of this earth or even of any of this material universe.

The true you is your mind (the Father), your spirit (the Mother), and your soul. Your soul is who you are, your individuality, your unique personality, the thing that makes you completely original. Your soul, or you, is made up of the true trinity. The true cross, not the crucifix, is the crossing of the Father and the Mother which makes the Son or Christ. Christ means the crossing of the Father and the Mother.

All that you are now wondering about will be explained. This extreme knowledge of truth will eventually blow you away. You will completely awaken from your unknowing sleep. You will become free from your entrapment. You will know everything and everything will know you. You will come to realize that you are far greater than time, darkness, sound, death and this whole material universe. Let us now get back to understanding the very beginning.

In the very beginning, the Father had his first thought, and this thought became his image. He gave his image a name and her name is MAN. She is the Holy Spirit.

Read the first gospel of John, which has been edited by religion, and not John I of John I, II and III, but the larger, first gospel of John. Remember to find and read from as old of the scriptures as you can, because throughout the years, the scriptures have changed more and more. Religion does this. You might like to know that a Jehovah Witness bible uses the oldest scriptures that have not been changed as much, because they believe extremely in Jehovah which is one of the many names of the god who is no more. You will find more accurate truth, believe it or not, in one of these bibles.

When you start to read from the first gospel of John you may see brackets around a word or some of the words. This means that they are not sure of the true words that go there or they don't want you to know. Regardless of this, read this scripture but replace the word god with the word MAN, which is the name of the Holy Spirit.

The Da Vinci Code and the Gnostics

The reason I ask you to do this is because this scripture is a Gnostic scripture whose author is not John but is Mary Magdalene.

This, I will have you know, is the true Da Vinci code. You see, in the painting of the Last Supper, Mary Magdalene is sitting in the so-called, "place of John". Mary Magdalene was the beloved disciple to Christ, not John. What? Was Christ gay? No he was not gay. Pay attention to this: "and the beloved disciple leaned his head upon Jesus' chest and said, 'Lord who is the one who will betray you?' And the Lord whispered into his

9

ear, 'it is the one who will dip his bread into the cup with me.'"
Leaned his head upon his chest? Whispered into his ear? This
sounds gay. It is because this disciple is a woman. A beloved
disciple could only be a woman. What Da Vinci is showing you
in his painting, is that everything that you read in the New
Testament that is authored by John is actually gospels of Mary
Magdalene. The authorship of the John Gospels has been
changed and the scriptures have been edited.

Getting back to the changing of the word god to MAN,
by changing the word god to MAN you can understand that
Mary Magdalene is speaking about the Holy Spirit, because the
Holy Spirit's name is MAN. By reading the gospel of John, in
this way, you will get a more true understanding of the very
beginning, which happened before the beginning of time and
material stated in Genesis.

What is a Gnostic scripture and who were the Gnostics?
A Gnostic scripture is a scripture written by the Gnostics who
were, Mary Magdalene and the Apostles, who were the first
Christians. Gnostic means, "One who knows."

Like I said, the Gnostics were the first Christians. They
were the Christians who were persecuted, who were crucified,
stoned to death, and burned alive. And guess who the ones who
persecuted them were. It was the Proto-Orthodox Christians.
These are the same Christians who exist today. Proto-Orthodox
means, "The Correct," or, "Right Ones." But they claimed
themselves to be the correct or right religion. As a matter of fact,
the Gnostics did not even claim to be a religion, because Christ
never wanted religion to come to be. He opposed it.

You see, religion wants you to believe, to have faith, to
hope, and to wish. Gnosis means to know. I ask you: would you
rather believe, have faith, hope, wish, or would you rather
KNOW?

Eternal Realm

The most important thing that we are to know is that we are from the very beginning and not from the beginning of time and material.

The very beginning is what brings forth the Eternal Realm. The Gnostics call this place, "The Pleroma." It is the true heaven. It is Eternal Life. It is never ending. Time does not exist there, and eventually we will all return to it.

Now, this is how it came to be, but remember, this material universe has existed for about 15 billion years, the Eternal Realm, or the Pleroma, which I am speaking of, has existed before this material universe and will continue to exist eternally even after this dead material universe is long gone.

Now, after the image of the Father (who is the first thought of the Father, who is the first to come forth, who is the Holy Spirit, whose name is MAN) came forth, she was then conceived by the Father, and after came forth the Son. Now, the name of the Son is, "Holy Man," or Christ. His name is Holy Man because the Father has no name therefore the only thing that he can be called is Holy, because he is perfect and is complete goodness. Christ means the crossing of the Father and the Mother. So then, if the Father is called Holy and the Mother is called MAN, then the Son's name is Holy Man.

Christ shows us that the Father's given name is Holy in a prayer called, "The Our Father" or "The Lord's Prayer." This prayer is actually a Gnostic prayer, but people do not know this. This will be explained later on in this book, but first let me show you how the Father's given name by Christ is Holy or Hallowed which means the same as Holy. It is revealed in the beginning of this prayer as such, "Our Father who art in heaven HALLOWED BE THY NAME."

Now that you know the name of the Son, the original Christ, I will continue. After Christ came forth, who is the Father and the Mother in one, he then created or brought forth, the first perfect MAN or next son of MAN along with the consort of the first perfect MAN. The name of the first perfect MAN that Christ brought forth is Adam, which also means Father. The name of his consort is Eve.

This Adam and Eve are not the same as the flesh Adam and Eve that were created from ash by god, the eleven other gods, and all the flesh angels in the material universe. This will be explained later on in this book, for we are still explaining the very beginning.

Before Christ brought forth Adam and Eve, he had the complete power of the Father and the Holy Spirit. From the Father he was given will, and of course, mind. From the Mother, he has forethought, foreknowledge, indestructability, eternal life, and truth. These are the first five powers belonging to the Holy Spirit. This is why the five pointed star is the symbol of the Holy Spirit. This is also why our material flesh bodies are in the shape of a five pointed star with our head at the top, our two arms and our two legs. We were made in the shape of MAN, her shape.

Christ, with these powers, breaks them down into three powers: the trinity powers. Will, the power of the Father, Thought, the power of the Mother, and Life the power of the Son. In this order it simply comes out as, "WILL THOUGHT LIFE." I hope you can understand.

Now let this not be complicated to you, but this is what happened next. With these powers or Aeons he brought forth the 12 perfect Aeons to bring forth, Adam and Eve, the son and daughter of Adam and Eve named Seth and Norea, the Children or Seed of Seth and Norea, whom amount in 120 children, 60

12

male and 60 female, and from these 120 Children of Seth came all the rest of the Children of Light, which are uncountable.

These are the 12 perfect powers used to bring us all forth. These powers are also called Aeons. The first is Grace, second is Form, and the third is Truth. These first three are where resides, Christ and Adam and Eve. The fourth is Perception, fifth is Conception, and sixth is Memory. These next three are where resides, Seth and Norea. The seventh is Understanding, eighth is Love, and ninth is Idea. These are where resides, the 120 Seed of Seth. Tenth is Perfection, eleventh is Peace, and twelve is Wisdom. These final Aeons are where resides, all the rest of the eternal Children of Light.

This is how the Eternal Realm or The Pleroma came to be from the very beginning. And all of us children of MAN existed there in peace and perfection long before this dead material universe came to be from a mistake that was forgiven.

In the Beginning of Time and Material
Out of Ignorance It Came

The beginning of time and material, which is this material universe, of which we are now living in, came to be out of Ignorance. This is why there is not one living thing here that ever knows why it is here, where it came from, or where it is going. Not even the first archon or god ever told us where he came from or how he came to be. And this god who came to be along with this material universe is not the Father of whom Christ speaks of.

I will now prove to you that he is not the Father. It is simple to understand. Moses wrote down what this god told him in a book called Genesis. And the first three words "IN THE BEGINNING" of this book tell you that he is not the Father. Do you know what the first three words "IN THE BEGINNING" of this book are? If you haven't figured it out by now, the first three words are "IN THE BEGINNING." You see, the Father doesn't have a beginning. This god said, "I am the Alpha and the Omega," which means the beginning and the end.

I spoke of earlier in the last chapter that the symbol representing the Holy Spirit was a five pointed star. Well the symbol for the Father is a circle or zero, for a circle has no beginning or end to it. It is timeless. This is one way to know that this god is not the Father. Also, since Christ is the Father and the Mother in one, then this symbol represents Christ ⊕. Does this symbol look familiar to you? The church or religion made this symbol out to be evil. They even said that it was the symbol of the devil. Many people on this planet pray to and worship a dead body nailed to a crucifix. A crucifix is not a cross. A cross is a plus sign + or an ×. A crucifix is a symbol of torture and death. How evil is that? Why would anyone want to

14

worship a crucifix? By the way, the devil is not who you think he is. I will explain this later.

Equality

Here is something important to know. Before this universe came to be, equality was set in motion. Every single male MAN has a female MAN consort. And they all are in need of each other. This is the only need that a true MAN has. But there is one who is not in need of a consort and that one is Christ. Why does Christ not need a consort? Because the Father's consort is the Holy Spirit, and since Christ is the Father and the Mother in one, he is not in need of a consort. But Christ chose a consort. He chose to be his consort the least of the twelve Eternal Aeons. You see, Christ is the greatest Aeon, Grace. He chose as his consort, Sofia, who is the eternal feminine Aeon, Wisdom, who is the least of the twelve. Why did he do this? Why did he choose the least? Because by blending the greatest with the least he established equality. That's why Christ calls us his brothers and sisters. He makes us all even equal to him.

By this you can understand just how great Christ truly is. He does not need us to worship him. He does not ask for praise, unlike this god who wanted and needed. This god wanted us to worship him. He needed us to call him god. Unlike him, Christ makes all the children of MAN equal.

Time and Material Came to Be

Now, here is how time and material came to be. While we were all living happily in the Pleroma or Eternal Realm, we were creating, engendering, and inventing because knowledge and everything else in the Pleroma is limitless, the consort of Christ decided to bring something forth. Little did she know that the something that she desired to bring forth was actually nothing or nothingness. Christ was aware of this and told Sofia to not bring that forth. But Sofia, being wise, (you see Wisdom

15

can make a mistake) she went ahead and brought it forth anyway without her Maleness, without the consent of her consort. Because she did not know what would happen, she engendered Ignorance. That is why this material universe and the god that came with it is Ignorant.

When this first archon, which means ruler, came forth, because before he came forth there was not rule, he was ignorant and did not know where he came from. His first appearance was like a serpent with the face of a lion. He thought he was the one and only. He also knew that he could mold and do with what he wanted the material that came with him, which is him. But then Sofia was moving to and fro, agitated in despair, so worried and ashamed of what she did. Moving to and fro above the waters, and above her now fatherless son, who, since then had thought he was the one and only, and called himself, "god," she then yelled out, "Yaltabaoth!" Which means, "Move from here to there." This word, "Yaltabaoth," was also the first sound and first verbal expression ever spoken. Because it was spoken in this material universe where sound exists, this word also became the first name of this first god. Later on this god received many other names such as, Allah, Jehovah, Yahweh, Elohim, and the All Mighty. These are the names given to him by religion. But before religion came, he had many other names as well.

The Root of All Evil

Getting back to his first name, when this god heard his mother speak from above him, he then knew he was not the one and only, that there was someone above him greater than him. This is the first thought of the material universe. He then engendered, Jealousy. You see, jealousy is the first dead Aeon to come forth in this material universe. It is the root of all evil, not money. Money does not have intelligence and is not an Aeon. Think about this. When a person obtains something of great

16

value like a house or a car or a ring or a watch, the first thought from other people is not happiness and joy for that person. No. The first thought, is jealousy. Then other dead powers or Aeons start to come.

Explaining Aeons

What is an Aeon? An Aeon is something that exists that you cannot see or touch. But it does exist. Like, love is an Aeon. Hate is an Aeon. You cannot see them but they do exist.

Learning about Aeons is the first step to becoming free from the corruption of this world. I mean, you can change your whole life. You can become the true person that you are. You can make anything happen. You can create your own life. You won't have to ever work for someone else ever again.

Ok, the Aeons in the Pleroma are all eternal, living Aeons. Some are male eternal Aeons and the opposite of them are female eternal Aeons. The Aeons in this material universe are not all eternal living ones. This is where you get the Yin and the Yang. Yin is eternal living Aeons and Yang is dead Aeons that are not eternal. In the Pleroma there is only Yin. In this place there is both Yin and Yang.

The first dead Aeon to come forth here is jealousy. Then all the other dead Aeons followed. You can do yourself good to be free of or get rid of the Aeon jealousy, since it is the first dead one. Then all the other ones will be that much easier to get rid of. Later on I will show you how you can destroy all of the dead Aeons. These dead Aeons are the reason why people can never be successful or accomplish their goals. Destroy the dead Aeons that hold you back. Have only living Aeons within you and be and do anything, and I mean anything.

Getting back to the first archon, the first ruler, the one who created the word and the meaning of the word god, and who called himself god, this first god created eleven other gods and countless flesh angels.

Gnostic Scriptures

You can find this information in the Gnostic scriptures. They are the first scriptures, the ones that have not been changed and the ones that religion and government do not want you to read. The thing is though, that almost all of them have been written in Apocrypha. Apocrypha means, "Hidden knowledge." Unless you can read Apocrypha, you cannot understand.

If you decide to read from them, I advise you to read from the books authored by Bart D. Ehrman. He does not try to change the meaning of them or try to tell you what he thinks they mean. He does his best to give you the exact translation into English. There are scholars today who are changing the meaning of them and are trying to give them to you in false interpretations, just like religion has been doing for the last 2,000 years.

When the Gnostics (the ones who know) wrote these first original scriptures, they wrote them in code or Apocrypha. Certain words stand for other words. For instance, bread can mean knowledge, or darkness can mean evil or the lack of good. And light, means mind.

Trapped Light

When Yaltabaoth came forth out of ignorance from the Pleroma, trapped light went with him. That same trapped light is all the Children of Light or Children of Mind or Children of the Father or Children of MAN, who are in bodies of human beings that live and die on this earth.

Until we become free from this material universe and its flesh, we will continue to live and die here over and over again. Believe it or not you can only leave from here while you are in a living body. How can you go to eternal life from death? This

18

makes no sense, because life begets life and death begets death. This is why Christ says," He who believeth upon me and dies shall live again and he who believeth upon me and lives shall never die."

The Twelve Gods

Now that you know how this 15 billion year old time and material universe of darkness, sound, and death came to be, let's make some sense of things.

After this god came forth, like scientists say from a big bang, (yeah this is how he came forth) he then created eleven other gods or archons. Then these twelve gods created a great multitude of flesh angels. There are two kinds of angels, spirit angels from the Pleroma and flesh angels from this universe.

After they created their flesh angels, these gods and angels formed this material universe. But they thought their intelligence made it all. No, the Holy Spirit worked through them to form this universe.

Now, there had to be an intelligence to form this universe. It could not just happen and I will prove it. First of all, let's be aware of something. What is the one thing that is eternal and indestructible in this universe? That one thing is water. You cannot destroy water. It is indestructible. And, it came from the Pleroma. That is why it is eternal. Everything else in this universe is dissolving away, stars are always burning up and the fire that is burning them up is burning out. New stars are not being born. Many of the stars that you see in the night sky are not even existent anymore.

Every galaxy has a giant black hole in the center of it, and the whole galaxy is slowly swirling into the black hole and being consumed. Even the false light from fire gets consumed by these black holes. And where is all this material going when it gets consumed by the black holes? It goes back to the Pleroma, back to where it came from, back to the Father, back to life. Nothing returns back to everything. Yes, this place is nothing because it ends, becoming something again.

Now that you know how the end to this universe is happening, let's speak of how life exists in this dead place. Know this. Life can exist in death but death cannot exist in life. When death is taken to life it becomes alive again.

Now I will show you how god did exist here. Okay, scientists are always trying to figure out how life began here. They seek the germ of life or first cell-like creatures. But this is not the root of life. The root of life is water. There must be liquid water for life to exist in this material universe.

The System of 12

Now I will explain something to you that no scientist ever thought of. I call this," The System of 12."

In order for life to exist here, there must be a System of 12. This is why there were twelve gods.

Look to all the different ancient civilizations. There were always 12 main gods. And these gods had faces and heads like animals. But the gods didn't look like animals. The gods made the animals to look like them. That's why the zodiac has twelve different kinds of animals representing them.

There are many other planets in this universe that have life on them. And many of these planets have our brethren on them, relative human beings or human kind. We call them aliens. Notice how aliens are always described having a head, two arms, and two legs. The five pointed star shape.

Well, like I said, without the System of Twelve, life cannot exist here. And all the other planets in this universe that sustain life are set up by the System of Twelve.

Here it is. For many years we thought that our solar system had nine planets orbiting the sun. This is not true. We actually have twelve. A System of 12 solar system could not just come to be. It is set up darn near perfect, even though this universe is not perfect. Well, the sun is a certain size and weight, and all the planets are a certain size and weight to make sure that the System of 12 works. And after I explain this you ought to see how this could not just come to be. Intelligence had to set it up and put it in motion. The planets all orbit the sun at a certain distance and a certain speed. This is all done this way just for the third planet Earth.

When you see an eclipse, solar or lunar, notice how whichever orb, the earth or the moon, blocks out the sun's light or the moon light perfectly. Neither one blocks it out larger or smaller. It is always blocked out in the same circumference as seen from here on earth. How could this just happen? Someone had to set this up just right. And I have just begun. The earth orbits the sun at a certain speed and distance to make sure that we have 12 months per year and the earth spins at a certain speed so that we have 12 hours per day and 12 hours per night. And all of this System of 12, 12 planets, 12 months, 12 hours, is set up for only one reason. That reason is liquid water.

There must be liquid water in order for life to exist in this universe. Scientists say there once was life on mars, nonsense. If you go up too high on a mountain on earth you could freeze to death. If you try to hang out in Death Valley, California you could die of heat exhaustion. If the earth is moved in closer to the sun, it will be too hot. If it is moved away it will be too cold. It is set just right. In fact if you offset it in any way what so ever you will disturb this System of 12. Life on Mars? Phooey. Without the System of 12, life cannot exist. And this is why there were 12 gods.

There is a group called the ancient alien theorists who think that the gods and the flesh angels were aliens. No. These ancient aliens that they speak of were in fact the 12 gods and the many flesh angels that did exist. And the aliens of today are human kind brethren from other life-giving planets, set up with the System of 12.

The Dragon

If you read from the Gnostic scriptures, you will find that the first appearance of the first god was like a serpent with the face of a lion.

Take a look at the Chinese dragon. This is exactly how it looks. As a matter of fact, the Chinese still, to this day, worship their god as this same dragon and believe that he still exists.

Scientists and people say that dragons never existed, but dinosaurs are all different kinds of dragons. They existed for millions of years.

The first appearance of the gods, before they started changing their appearances to look more like MAN, was that of dragons or serpents or giant reptiles. They created these dinosaurs, having fun with them, doing gene manipulation, competing with each other, and seeing who could make the best of the dinosaurs. It was many billions of years before they ever saw or even knew about MAN.

Look throughout all of the ancient civilizations and you will see dragons everywhere. After dragons, came mammals. The gods began changing their appearances. Come on, they are material and material is them. Flesh is material and flesh can be manipulated.

Material and Time Must Finish

You see, time and material cannot just be stopped. It has to play itself out. So, the Holy Spirit knows the right time to do certain things.

Notice that hominids, or the early so-called "caveman", never really evolved. They always changed from one kind of so-called caveman into another more intelligent caveman overnight. This is also gene manipulation.

Millions of years ago, god was going around bragging to all the other gods and flesh angels, that he was the one and only god because he made all the others and that he was not in need of anything. At this time, the Holy Spirit shined above them all. They all saw her and she spoke, "there is one before you. This one is MAN."

When god said let us make a MAN in our image, how did they know what a man looked like? Where did they even get the word MAN from? And why did it take so many millions of years for them to decide to make one anyway? It's because the Holy Spirit chose the right time to show herself. They saw her so they tried to make a copy of her in their image. It took them millions of years of trying.

If you look in Genesis in the bible you will see that they created humans before they created Adam and Eve. Human beings, (human meaning upright walking man) were living here on planet earth. Adam and Eve, the flesh Adam and Eve, were created on another planet called Paradise.

The reason for 12 different gods and so many flesh angels is because of the distribution of Aeons. The many different Aeons like, love, hate, wealth, poverty, joy, sorrow, kindness, meanness, and so on and so on, were distributed throughout the different gods and flesh angels. No one god or angel ever had all the Aeons in them. Let me show you.

For instance, a dog has three main Aeons: Jealousy, pet another dog and watch how jealous your dog gets, Greed, try to take a bone away from them, and Loyalty, your dog will attack and fight to the death to protect you. All animals have different Aeons in them just like the gods that made them.

The gods for a long time could not make a good enough human. So they decided to all of them, gods and flesh angels, to come together to make a human. And they did it on a planet called Paradise. The Holy Spirit set all of this up this way so that we can eventually be free from here sooner. After they all made Adam's body he didn't move for a long time. Then a spirit angel disguised as a flesh angel told god to breathe into the nostrils of Adam, since he is the almighty, then Adam will rise. Well, sometime in the far past, god had taken the breath of life from his mother Sofia. But being arrogant, god foolishly blew the breath of life into Adam. Adam then rose and was luminous. He had all of the Aeons in him because he was created by them all. He was now far more intelligent than all of the gods and the flesh angels. He was even far more intelligent than the first main god Yaltabaoth.

The gods and the flesh angels were all extremely angry that they were tricked, but they could not yet kill Adam. They tried to take life from him by creating a female man from his rib DNA. Now we have Adam and Eve.

The Tree of Death and the Tree of Knowledge

I will now show you the mystery of the two trees in Paradise, the so-called tree of life and the tree of knowledge.

When god realized that the breath of life was lost to him and was now within Adam and Eve, he also discovered that at that time Adam and Eve were the only two beings in material that had eternal souls. This god did not have an eternal soul, and of course could not create an eternal soul. So he hated these two children of MAN. And he will also continue hating all the descendants of the children of MAN, thereafter. Just read from the Old Testament and you will see all of the wonderful things that he did to us (sarcasm).

Now since he hated us so much, here is the mystery of what he did with the two trees in Paradise. He wanted to deceive Adam and Eve, so he set up a garden place on Paradise and made it out to be so wonderful and nice so as to con Adam and Eve. There he set up two trees of fruit making them look so desirable. One of the two trees was called the Tree of Life. Pay attention to how I say "called." This tree was actually a tree of death. The other tree was the Tree of Knowledge or of knowing and little did god know was that the Holy Spirit worked through him to set up this tree.

Here is the con game that god played on them, and he said, "Of all of the fruit and of the vegetation in the Garden of Eden, thou mayest eat. But of the fruit from the Tree of Life and the fruit from the Tree of Knowledge thou shalt not eat." Well, if you were Adam or Eve and you knew that if you ate from the Tree of Life then you would supposedly live forever, why then would god make that tree so available for them to eat from it? It's because it was actually a tree that would kill them. It was a tree of death.

He tried to be tricky or deceptive. But Christ came to them as an eagle and not as a serpent. Well also remember that god is the first serpent. Hm, who really is the devil here? Anyway, coming to them as an eagle, Christ told Eve (knowing that the female MAN was much stronger than the male MAN) to eat from the Tree of Knowledge so that she could KNOW!

Christ, knowing that she is much stronger, chose her also because he knew of the great terror and horror that the female MAN will have to go through throughout the coming ages. You see, the male MAN would not be able to bear what the female MAN will be able to endure and survive from.

By the way, if you cut an apple in half sideways, you will find that inside there will be revealed to you a five pointed star.

After this, god was extremely angry and took them out of Paradise and put them on a planet down into the farthest part of Tartarus, which is this planet called Earth. This happened exactly 120,000 years ago from the date 2012, December 21st. By the way, Christ came here exactly 2,000 years ago from this date. So Christmas could be celebrated on the 21st of December and not the 25th.

Pay attention to this number 120. It is mentioned often since before time and throughout time. Worry not, I will show this all to you. Even scientists say that Cro-Magnon man made his beginning here on earth around 120,000 years ago. Cro-Magnon man is the same human that lives today. And the first two Cro-Magnon men were Adam and Eve.

Children of MAN Become Human Beings

As I mention earlier, human means man walking upright. Every man of whom anyone has ever known of has always walked upright. So why do we say man and human? How many people have ever thought about this? The difference is that MAN who existed before human did not ever need to walk. Human is physical and walks upright. But eternal MAN, need not walk, nor does MAN need a physical body.

The Holy Spirit made sure that the gods would make a human being that would have all of the Aeons in it before she put into it the soul of eternal MAN. That way, eventually MAN in the human form would come to know everything here as well as everything of the eternal realm.

This is what means the "here and now." Here means this material place where we are. Now means the eternal realm. You see, since the eternal realm has no time in it, it's always now. But people do not understand the difference of time and eternity, even though they are in both places at once.

I will show you. Know this that you can never be in the past and you also can never be in the future. You can always only be in the now. For you it is always now. When you wake up tomorrow it will be now. Therefore time does not even really exist. Time and material cannot exist without a beginning and an end. So when you can understand the now, that you are always in, then you will know that you are in both places. And since this place does not really exist, because eventually it will all return to the kingdom of heaven, or the eternal realm, then you will understand that you are always in the kingdom of heaven and that the kingdom of heaven is always in you.

Creation can only come from the now or from the kingdom of heaven or from the eternal realm. All of which are the same place so always think from the now so that your future will turn out the way that you will it to. Learn how to use this great power. Learn how to use this real magic. Oh yes the kingdom of heaven is truly here and now. This simple knowledge is unknown to everyone here on earth. They are always thinking of the past and of the future that have no existence. This is one reason why they are always lost and miserable.

Now that you know why the Holy Spirit did what she did, I will continue. The flesh Adam and Eve knew that they were far more intelligent than all of the gods and the flesh angels. So they had to be careful not to anger them. After the gods saw MAN, the Holy Spirit, who showed herself to them, they then finally made physical man, a male and a female in their image. So what we look like now, or what our bodies look like, is all of the gods and the angels put together.

Well, after that, the gods started to change their appearances again keeping the way that their heads and faces looked, but changing their bodies to look like ours. You can see these depictions in many ancient civilization paintings. Ancient paintings on Egyptian walls are a good example. They did this because they thought that if they could become like us, they could also become eternal. So they thought.

The gods did many things to try to become like us. Especially inter breeding. This first occurred after flesh Adam and Eve were created. What I am about to tell you now may sound shocking but I am fearless and am not afraid to tell the truth. Before Adam and Eve ever had sex together or mated the first god or Yaltabaoth took Eve. Being ignorant, he thought he could generate an eternal child, but material or flesh is not eternal, and all that this god was, was material flesh. Even his soul was not eternal.

So, you could say that he raped Eve. He did this twice. And Eve gave birth to two sons. The first was Cain and the second was Abel. You see, at this time Children of Light still had a united mind. And I will explain this later. But by having a united mind one would not kill or do any evil thing. What happened between these two children of god was this: Abel taunted Cain by bragging that his burnt offering to their father was greater than his. Because of this Cain killed him.

God engendered killing since the beginning of time and material. Every so called living thing that god ever made is always killing another living thing to survive. How imperfect is this? How good is this? You see god was never good, that's why he has always been missing an o.

Here is some more proof of this. If Cain was the son of Adam don't you think god would have killed him? God wiped out whole civilizations just because they would not worship him. God killed many times for many reasons sometimes just to do it. Just read the bible and see for yourself. He even made a commandment that stated, "Thou shalt not kill." "I may kill" but "thou shalt not." God did not want to kill his only son born from an eternal female MAN, no matter what bad thing his son did.

And now I will show you another mystery. God said that he put a mark on Cain. Well, he did not need to put a mark on him. Cain was born with this mark. Remember how god came forth with the body of a serpent and the face of a lion? A lion is a certain kind of cat, a cat face. Well, Cain is an Asian name. And all Asians have the face of a cat. Also god made sure that the Asians were the most populated people on the earth. The Asians to this day still worship, as I said earlier, the dragon as their god. All Asian bodies are descended from Cain.

Notice how I say, "bodies." Eventually, quite soon as a matter of fact, the Asian's bodies were incased with the souls of

29

the Children of Light. Even though their bodies descend with their faces looking like god, the men inside their bodies are our brethren Children of Light. Also remember this. All material flesh is of god. We are not our bodies. We are not of god. So the favorite people of god were not the Israelites, but the Asians.

After Cain and Abel, Adam and Eve finally began to mate and their first son was Seth. Just like the order in the Pleroma. Throughout history god tried to destroy the Children of Seth but they survived through Lot and his daughters.

But before I go on, I will reveal something to you. The bible is kind of like a history book. Pay attention to this. Doing research and using common sense, I have come to know that there have been four ages of MAN kind. Other prophets, the Mayan, the Hopi Indians and others have this as a belief also. Well I happen to know that the beginning of the fourth age of which we are at the end of now, soon to be over on the date 2012, December 21st, started at the time of the great flood, the flood that covered the whole earth, wiping out almost all intelligent life on planet earth, the flood where Noah survived with the building of a great ark. Well, Noah had a lot of help from the first god and the flesh angels.

Regardless of this, at this time I will show you something. Get a bible. Open to the page in Genesis where it is written about the great flood. With your right hand, place your thumb on the inside of the book on the right side page. And let your fingers be on the other outside part of the book at the back end. And with your left hand, hold the other front side of the book the same way. You will then notice that from the flood to the end of the book is almost the whole book. And from the beginning of the book to the great flood is hardly any of the book at all.

Well from the flood to the end of the book is all of this 4th age of which I estimate to be thirty thousand years. And from Adam and Eve to the flood are the first three ages of mankind of which I estimate to be 90 thousand years. I come to this estimation by dividing up the ages by 30 thousand years each. If mankind has been here for 120 thousand years, from Adam and Eve to 2012, December 21st, I then simply divide them up into four equal parts of 30 thousand years each.

What I'm getting at is this, the smallest part of the book is the longest that we have been here. This is how much we do not know of our past. People think that we are at our most intelligent era of mankind. This is not true. We have diminished. We were far more intelligent and did much greater things. And most important of all, we were much more united.

Here is something I will show you. Look to the beginning of god's book, the bible, and check out the first paragraph. Remember that god said that he was the one and only god, meaning that he was the first. Yes he was the first god. Then he says, "And thou shalt have no other gods before me." He is saying that there were other gods just don't put them before him. Well, if he was the one and only and came before eternal MAN, then in his first paragraph who is the spirit moving to and fro above him and above the waters? If he is the one and only then why would his spirit be somewhere else? I'll tell you why, because he had no spirit. And the one moving to and fro above the waters, above him, is his mother the Aeon Wisdom named Sofia.

Now let me show you this. God lies and says that he made the earth in six days. Yeah right, when we know that the universe is like 15 billion years old. And this solar system is also about 5 billion years old.

31

Notice that when he speaks of the sun and the moon he calls them luminaries. Luminaries are lights that glow through something. Now he does speak a tiny bit about the stars but that's only because he is speaking to Moses. And in Moses' time, the stars could be seen. But in the time of Adam, up until the flood, the earth was completely covered with clouds all the time. That's why he called the sun and the moon luminaries.

Pay attention. He says, "I will put a firmament between the waters." The firmament is the space above the waters on the earth and is below the waters above. The waters above are the clouds. He called the firmament, which is the space containing air under the clouds, heaven. Well, he did this because he didn't want us to know that there was a universe outside of earth's atmosphere. That's why he lied about creating the earth in six days.

Well the gods and the flesh angels mingled with the humans throughout the first three ages. They taught the humans many things. Remember that the gods and the flesh angels could travel the universe that humans didn't know about. But whatever the humans learned from the gods, they perfected that knowledge and made everything they learned even greater. The reason why the gods mingled with us is because they hoped to become eternal like us. But this could never happen so instead they ruled over us and mistreated us.

Look at the descriptions and the images of the kings of old. Notice how they are always larger than the humans being ruled by them. It is because the gods and the flesh angels mated with the daughters of MAN. When they did this children were born to them half god or angel and half human. These were called the Nephilim. They were giants. And the gods always made sure that the ruling kings were these Nephilim. That is why kings always said that they were descendants of the gods, because they were. Also, all ancient civilizations sacrificed their own brethren of mankind to the gods. The gods wanted the blood of human beings to pour for them.

There are many remembered names of these Nephilim: Samson, Goliath, Aquiles, Hector, and Hercules. Read again in Genesis and you will find a passage that reads, "The sons of the first god began to notice the daughters of man that they were good-looking and they went taking wives for themselves, namely, all whom they chose." Notice the word taking. This so-called god is supposed to be good, isn't he? Why is he letting his flesh angel sons take our women for sex just because our women are good looking?

Now go ahead and read chapter six of Genesis. Now remember that we were dominated by eternal Aeons. We came from the place of the eternal living Aeons. The sons of god are from this place of dead evil Aeons. So these giants that came forth, who were half flesh angel and half human, were terrible. They wreaked havoc on the whole earth. They were the ones whose fault it was that the world became extremely wicked. But as you read on you will see that god blamed us. It was his sons that caused all the evil, not us.

That's when he decided to flood the whole earth and destroy all the horror that was going on by bringing the waters from above the firmament down upon the earth. Remember that up to this time the waters or thick clouds did not allow us to see outer space. Well the ark of Noah had DNA of much of the animal life on earth, male DNA and female DNA, two of many species of animals. The gods and the flesh angels knew how to create and to preserve animal life. Come on, they are the masters of material and flesh.

Pay attention to this. After the flood, god told Noah that he would give him a great sign that would show that god would

33

never flood the earth again. The sign was a rainbow, but a rainbow only shows when the sun is shining. Also, he couldn't flood the earth again. What was he going to do, make all that water that it took 40 days and nights to flood the whole earth, go back into the sky? I mean, these clouds were so thick no one could ever see the stars. He could not flood the earth again if he wanted to.

Ok, these ancient aliens, who were actually gods and flesh angels, controlled and ruled us for 118 thousand years, until Christ came and got rid of all of them. Where are they now?

Now I will show you something else. The greatest city that ever existed on this planet was a city called Re'sen. Remember we are the children of MAN. The greatest essence of the Holy Spirit is water. Our greatest power energy source was crystalline power. Notice the name, "Cryst"al power. Crystals and water go together. That's why the Holy Spirit made sure we had the moon. Without the moon our oceans would be way out of control. You see, the moon is a giant crystal. Look at the moon compared to all other planets and other moons. It is the only orb in the sky that shines like a glass ball. Yes, we took our power from the moon, using crystals here on earth.

Now the city of Re'sen was not on land. It was a great floating city. It was the biggest city ever. It was set up between two continents. And it had another well-known name. That name is Atlantis. How ridiculous is it that people wonder where Atlantis was? Duh, the Atlantic Ocean. The bible even has written in it about Atlantis or the great city Re'sen

Atlantis had a great king, the greatest king that ever lived. He was a good king and this king was so great that he opposed Jehovah, god, or Yaltabaoth. God feared him and could never kill him. To this day there is no evidence of his death. His name was Nimrod.

34

If you read chapter eleven in Genesis, you will see for yourself that at that time we inhabited the whole earth, we were one united human race, we all spoke one language. We spoke to each other with our minds. God even says in this chapter that there is nothing that they may have in MIND to do that will be unattainable for them. We built a tower that would reach the heavens or that would take us through outer space.

We built many of these towers that had great crystals on top of them. Many of these towers still stand today. They are the great pyramids and they are all over the earth. You see, from a System of 12 planet human beings cannot venture out in to space if they are divided and in conflict with each other. So-called aliens of today travel the universe because they are at peace with each other. They are a different human kind and they are our brethren. In this era of mankind on earth we were united, we loved each other. We were one race of mankind looking all different as we do now.

You see, in this material universe, when living Aeons and dead Aeons are together then the living Aeons dominate over the dead ones and the dead ones have no power. This is why we could all speak with our minds. We had nothing to hide, no person had evil intent, and because of this we were united.

The gods knew that we were about to leave our atmosphere. They said that we will be like them. Like them meaning, that we will be able to travel the universe as they did. So what did god do? He divided the Aeons in our brains giving us left brain with the dead Aeons and right brain with the living Aeons. Because of this we could not communicate with each other like we used to. Now that the Aeons were divided, evil or corruption obtained power. We became divided and started different cultures throughout the earth. We had to start talking vocally with many different languages for all the many different

35

cultures. We became enemies of each other. We have been warring, murdering, raping, enslaving, and destroying each other ever since god did this to us until now. Since then until now, the only ambition that has been for human kind on this earth was to conquer and rule. What more need be said about mankind here on earth? You know all the rest. All the rest, that is, up until when the original Christ came. And I will explain that in the chapter titled, "The Son."

Understanding the Father
How I Came to Know

I came to know the Father and the understanding of the Father with help from a book called, "The Secret of the Ages."

One day I was feeling bad. Things were not going well for me. So I reached for the bible. I put it down in front of me. But this time I didn't say god. I just looked at this book. Then I looked up and all around me. I then closed my eyes and said," Whoever you are, whatever you are, I know that there is a supreme source for everything and I wish you would just show me how to know the true you."

Then the next day a movie came on called, "Stigmata." And it spoke about a scripture called, "the Gospel of Thomas." And that in this gospel were the exact words that Christ said and Thomas wrote down. So then if this were true, then this gospel was not a gospel of Thomas, but a gospel of Christ. I also found out that Thomas was Jesus' brother. Well, if this is true, then why am I reading from Mathew, Mark, Luke, and John who only knew Christ as Jesus for a short time when he was like 30 years old, when Thomas would have known him his entire life? And why is this gospel not in the bible?

So I went looking for this gospel. I couldn't find it anywhere. Somehow weeks later I was in an old gold mine town called Oatman, Arizona where there was a library with really old books in it. I thought that just because it was old I might find the gospel there. Instead, I stumbled upon a book called, "The Secret of the Ages." I started reading a little, and then bought the book for 4 dollars. This book is worth millions. The Father directed me to this book. Robert Collier, the author of this book, knew and understood the Father, but he did not know exactly that the Father was not god. He also did not know of the Mother. But because of his book, I learned to go inside myself to know that the Father was inside me and not outside myself where everyone else keeps on looking. The Father is the secret. And the Mother is the truth.

First I found the Father and then I found the Mother. You can't have Christ without them both. Simply put, the Father is MIND. Your mind, everyone's minds, all mind. And we, the Children of Light (remember that light means mind) are the only living beings with eternal mind within us.

The Three Minds of the Father

I will now introduce you to yourself. Have you ever heard the term, know thyself? Well knowing thy self is knowing the Father who is within you. And because of this material place, he is split up within and without you.

To your complete mind, there are 3 parts. The first is your conscious mind or outer mind. It is only 10% of your complete mind. When you are talking with someone, when you are thinking about what to do or where to go, this is your outer mind. And it is polluted with dead Aeons. It is connected with this material place, divided from your inner mind. Everyone here does everything from this lesser of our complete minds. This mind is loaded with dead Aeons like failure, doubt, worry, discouragement, and so on, which makes it almost impossible for anyone to ever be happy.

Then there is your subconscious mind, which is the inner 90% of your complete mind. This inner mind is perfect and unpolluted. It has only eternal living Aeons in it. As a matter of fact, dead Aeons cannot exist in it. It is the greatest part of you. It knows no limits being eternal. It can make anything happen. It is part of your inner self, and it will make happen whatever your outer mind tells it to make happen. You see, because people do not know of it, they tell it to do mostly things that will make them fail. And so it gives power to failure.

Suggestion is what commands it. When you know thy self, or your inner mind, then you know that whatever you make your inner mind believe, your inner mind will then make happen. Make it believe that you are a loser then you will lose. Make it believe that you are a winner, and then you will win. Make it believe that you are poor, and then you will dwell in poverty. Make it believe that you are rich, and then you will be wealthy. Make it believe that you are sick then you will be weak. Make it believe you are healthy then you will be strong.

So then when you come to know yourself, then it's up to you to be what you will. Your inner mind listens to everything you think or say. It does not think. It only listens. What you believe in, it makes to be. So then think only goodness, think only prosperity. Convince it of only good things and good things will be. Let me give you an example of how it works. Pay attention to what happens to someone when they will say,"Damn it, this always happens to me!" The inner mind says,"Ok." And so the thing of which they do not desire keeps happening because they have convinced their inner mind that it keeps happening. And you've heard someone say, "I'm always lucky at this and I always win." Even other people give this person power by agreeing that this is true for him. And so the inner mind, being convinced of this, makes it so.

Now convincing your inner mind of things by believing in things is a powerful way to make things happen for you and to make things go your way. But it is far greater and more powerful to KNOW of things rather than to believe. Know you are rich. Know you are healthy. Know you are happy. Remember the great saying is to "Know thy self," not believe.

And now I will show you an even greater power. Remember how I said earlier that dead Aeons cannot exist in your inner mind, called the subconscious? Well, when you understand what indestructability is, you can become a superman. Pay attention. Super or supreme, the Supreme Being is the Father of whom is the mind within you. And MAN is the Holy Spirit. If your inner mind is of the supreme, dead Aeons cannot exist there. If you could take your outer mind and bring it into your inner mind, than all of the pollution corrupting your outer mind that makes you think in a negative way, would be destroyed. Remember when I said that life can live in death but death cannot live in life? Well, your outer mind has living Aeons living among dead ones. Life is living in death. But your inner mind can have only living Aeons in it. So then I say again, bring the outer mind in. Have the ability to destroy from within. Destroy from within the dead Aeons. In-destruct-ability, destroy corruption and become irresistible. Destroy the resistance that once did stop you.

All that I have explained is broken down to these two things: Convince "thy self" that "you are" and take "it" to yourself. Thy self is your inner mind. "It" is the dead Aeons. So bring the dead Aeons in to your inner mind.

I will go a little further with this second thing to show you more. You have heard, "Eat the body of Christ." Well your body is material flesh. Dead Aeons exist only because of material. So then, take the dead material Aeons in and eat them alive. Resolve them into their root. Bring them back to where they came from. Change them back into living Aeons by consuming them by bringing them in.

Now the third part of your mind is the greatest of all. It is all of the Father. It is every bit of him that is limitless. It is the mind of everyone and everything of which you are connected to.

40

Think of your conscious and subconscious minds as a drop of water having the same properties as the ocean. Then think of the super conscious mind as the ocean having the same properties as a drop of water. The two are the same. The difference is only in volume. So when you can connect your mind (the drop of water) with the super conscious mind (the ocean) you will then truly become a limitless, unstoppable, unconquerable, completely successful, superman with the ability to do anything what so ever. And I mean anything. But the first step to becoming this is to unite your conscious and subconscious minds first.

I will now show you something Gnostic unknown to all. Have you heard how when after many people pray they always say Amen? Why do they say this? They don't even know why or what they are saying. This is old Gnostic powerful magic, yes a true magic saying. Here is the true power and reason of this saying: A, meaning Adamas, or Adam which means Father, and MEN meaning all of the eternal Children of MAN, all of them or us, all of us here and all of us who are in the eternal realm. Or look at it this way. MEN of Adamas or all the men of the Father. The reason one would say this is because after one would pray for the thing desired, he would then unite himself and the conviction of his prayer with the whole eternal realm of all his brethren or all of the Father. This would give his prayer an extreme eternal power. With this much power, when one knows what one is saying and not just saying something just for the heck of it, one could do things like raise someone from the dead or turn water into wine or do anything. This would be the connection of the drop of water to the ocean. Know what Amen means. Do not just say it. Connect your mind with the mind of the Father.

41

Understanding the Mother

"Know thy self," and, "by self be known." This means know the Father and then the Father will know you. The Father is the source of everything and everything is the Mother.

So, when you know everything then everything knows you.

The Mother, more so known as the Holy Spirit, is the first thought of the Father. So if thought was first and mind is source then think of her as thought and the Father as mind from where thought first came.

I will now explain more of what I have told you earlier. She has 5 powers. And these are the first powers to come forth.

The first of course is thought, but because it came before everything else it is Forethought. Her second power is Foreknowledge, meaning to know before. Her third is Eternal Life, meaning that she lives eternally. The fourth is Indestructability, meaning she cannot be destroyed. And the fifth is truth. She is complete truth. In her, lies are non-existent.

Because of these five powers the five pointed star is her symbol. Also this is her shape. This is why we, her children whose bodies we are trapped in, were made to have her shape.

Now, because the Father and the Mother are the two in one making the Christ or the Son, I will show you that these great powers each have two meanings. The first, forethought, is this: fore, meaning before, is the power of the Father and thought, the power of the Mother. The second, foreknowledge, is this: fore of course means before, being the Father's power and knowledge, being the Mother's. Since the Father was not known the Mother makes it possible for him and all things to be known. Eternal life being the third is this: the Father is eternal and because of the Mother, comes forth life. The fourth is this: the Father's meaning was explained in the last chapter as the ability

42

to destroy from within, and the meaning for the Mother is that she cannot be destroyed. She is invincible. And the fifth power, truth, represents the Father and the Mother. The Father is true and the Mother is true. But the Mother is most represented as the truth. The reason being is that because of her the truth can be known. The truth will set you free! When you know these first five powers of truth, then you know the greatest magic of all.

Many millions of people, mostly women, were murdered mostly by being burned to death by religion because they knew about this truth. This happened mostly during the middle Ages. This knowledge came from a group of people in France who were taught this true knowledge by none other than Mary Magdalene herself. These people were called the Cathar, and they were the first to be burned alive by the Inquisition of the Roman Catholic Church. After them, millions were burned to death being called witches.

The Roman Catholics and all other so called Christians of today all derive from the Proto-Orthodox so called Christians. These murderers were and still are not true Christians. The Gnostic Christians were the only true ones. True Christians do not kill. Only god children kill.

The Holy Spirit is our Mother, the Mother of the eternal living ones. Her name is MAN. If you are still confused then I will explain more clearly to help you see.

When you see a dog it is either a female dog or a male dog. When you see a cat it is either a female cat or a male cat. So, when you see a MAN it is either a female MAN or a male MAN. We say Mankind. We do not say oh yeah and womankind too.

The word woman came from womb man. It was created to diminish the female MAN. Throughout history the female MAN was kept down and made to be less equal to the male

MAN. This is because god hated and was extremely jealous of the Holy Spirit who god knew was female. He hated Eve because she was the first in this material universe to come to know by eating from the Tree of Knowledge. This is why religion, whom loves the dead god, tries to say that the Holy Spirit is a male. Know this that any entity or any organization who chooses to put women or the female MAN beneath the male and try to make them less equal to the male MAN must be evil. Here are the three biggest entities that do this: secret societies, government, and religion.

Now I will show you the mystery of her name. It is the trinity. The first letter M represents the Mother. Notice how an M has five points. An M also is a five pointed star M M ⋈. The letter A stands for the Father. An A also has five points and is also a five pointed star A A A. The N represents the Son or Christ. An N is two triangles that mirror each other meaning the two in one, N ◰ ◰. MAN.

Now I will show you her power. When you use foreknowledge then you know what the future is. When you use forethought then you can change the future. Or with forethought alone you can create the future.

The Mother's essence is water. Water is her and she is water. Water is eternal and indestructible. Freeze water and it just turns to ice. Try to burn it, it just turns to steam. Pollute it and it will evaporate, leaving the pollution behind becoming pure again.

One of the biggest lies on this earth is that there is a water shortage. Such bull! The same water that has always been on this earth is the same water that is here now. It cannot go anywhere. It is also always the same amount. And it is a major

44

shame that people have to pay for it. All the trillions of dollars spent on technology and weapons and governments will not even purify our tap water.

Now here is the greatest part of her power. Remember she is the image of the Father. Then she is the image of the mind. So then she is the images in your mind. Use this power that is within you. Know that the images in your mind are the Holy Spirit within you. Image the things from the here and now that you will to happen in your life. For example, you desire a certain thing like a car. Image that car in every detail in your mind's eye. Convince your inner mind that you have this image and you will manifest it here on earth.

Circumstance is created by thought imaged in mind. Material is like clay that the images in your mind bring into being on this earth from the here and now. You cannot deny this. Everything that ever comes into being came from a thought first. Every invention, every building, every idea came first from a thought. Someone first thought the thing that has come into being as material here on earth.

Know that you are greater than material that you have existed before material, that you are the master of it and not the other way around. Material has no intelligence. You are intelligence. Know who you are. Be who you are.

The Son

The Son of MAN. I am the son of MAN. You are the son of MAN. We are all the sons and daughters of MAN. Simply put, the Son is the Father and the Mother in one. The Son completes the true trinity. The Christ is the Son. Christ means the crossing of the Father and the Mother, making the Son.

The original Son is within all of us but he is divided. The Father and the Mother are apart from each other within us. The Father is mind (light), and the Mother is spirit (water). We must bring them together as one. We must obtain the resurrection. But be not misled. This must be done while one is in a living body. A dead body has nothing in it. And bringing a dead body back to life is not the resurrection. Returning to the Pleroma or the eternal realm from a living body, this is the resurrection.

So far, there has only been one who has truly resurrected and it was not the original Christ, the one whom people call Jesus, which by the way is an English name. The original Christ, when he was with us in a physical form here on earth, was called Yeshua.

First know this: it is not possible for the Christ to die. Remember he is the Father and the Mother in one. If he died everything and nothing could not exist, everything being the eternal realm and nothing being this place.

Now here is one of the greatest mysteries of all. What I am about to tell you now one must be completely fearless to say. And since I am, then I will tell you. Mary Magdalene was the greatest Apostle of all. She was the most favorite of Christ. She was called his beloved. In the Gnostic gospel of Phillip, she is even called his lover. Knowing this it is then not hard to understand why the church or religion tried to diminish her and make her out to be a prostitute. I will show you who Mary Magdalene is and why Christ loves her so much.

Mary Magdalene is the one who was forgiven, the one who out of ignorance brought forth this dead material universe and the god of whom it belonged to. This god was her fatherless son. And he was the source of this oblivion.

After she (Sofia) was forgiven for what she had done, she now then had to undo what she had done. She had to rectify her deficiency. So she came here at the appointed time as Mary Magdalene. But when she came here she would not know who she was because of this place being from ignorance. And there could only be one who would be able to come here and be able to know. That one is Christ. So he followed his chosen consort and at the appointed time he met up with her here to show her why she came and what must be done. The source of her mistake, this oblivion, this chaos, must be removed. Her son Yaltabaoth the origin of death himself must die.

You see, there never was a devil. The devil was invented so that people would look to another for all the evil corruption of this place. And even if there was a devil then the fault would lie in the one who made him, but the only devil was god himself. Religion has always tried to make Christ and god to be as one. But they are certainly not. God wants you to fear him. Christ says fear not. God killed and murdered without question. Christ never killed and does not kill. God said to love the world. Christ says hate the world. God gave many commandments and from them came so many rules. Christ gives only one commandment: love thy brother and thy sister as thy self. You see if we all do this we are not in need of any other rules. Christ and god are not as one. As a matter of fact Christ came here around two thousand years ago to get rid of him.

47

Be aware of this, that the most popular person to ever be on this earth was Christ, who was called Jesus. But no one does not know what he looked like. The paintings of what have been made of him to look like are not what he looked like. He is not a body. He is the Christ of who can take any form. Why do you think Judas had to kiss the cheek of a person so that the Roman soldiers would know who to seize?

Ok, here we go. Remember that before Christ Jesus went to the Mount of Olives he could never be captured no matter what he did or where he was? And remember at the last supper he said, "This is my body which will be given up for you. And this is my blood which will be given up for you." He said his body and his blood will be given up, not Him.

Here is what happened. When he went to the Mount of Olives he then transformed. He then left that body which was called, "the lamb of god." You see a lamb is an animal that is most associated with being slaughtered, or sacrificed. Notice, "the lamb of god." Not the lamb of Christ. He left that body, the lamb of god, and put Yaltabaoth or god into it.

Now, this so called Jesus was different. He now gets down on his knees and asks that the things that are about to happen to not take place. Why would the original Christ ask such a thing? Christ is fearless and cannot die. This new Jesus was Yaltabaoth finally admitting that there is the Father far greater than him. And notice who is in the heavens among the clouds. It is Moses, Enoch, and Elijah. These three did not know Christ but they knew god. God extended their lives because he favored them. They are here at this time wondering what god is doing and why he is in this body.

Soon after the Roman soldiers took him quite easily, but except Judas must point him out with a kiss. Judas was not a traitor he was the one to point out the lamb of god. Peter is the traitor, for he denied Christ three times before the cock crowed. These three denials are the three great corrupt religions that Peter brought forth: Judaism, Islam, and the so called Christianity all of whom worship this dead god.

You see, Christ did not kill god. He only put him into this body that was brought forth for the purpose of getting rid of god. It was god's own children who killed him thinking that they were killing Jesus. "And god said, 'Forgive them Father for they know not what they do.'" And when he died he ripped the great curtain in two that was on the great temple. The Jews made this great curtain for god not Jesus. And who was there with her son as he dies? It was Mary Magdalene, his mother, who is also the disciple, who was there.

Remember there were 11 other gods. Well, of the twelve apostles, Judas is not spoken of anymore. In fact, it is said that he killed himself. That leaves the other 11 disciples, who were all also killed. Their purpose was to do the same thing as Christ did and replace their souls with the souls of the 11 other gods, to put them into their bodies that they be killed and be rid of.

You see, before Christ came two thousand years ago, it was the gods and the kings who ruled. After the gods were taken out, then the Kings lost their power. So then, religion took the place of the gods and government took the place of the kings.

After all this, Mary Magdalene went to France to teach the Cathar the truth. Then she became as Christ. Becoming a light water soul and she resurrected back to the Pleroma. She is the first and only one to resurrect. She did not die. And you can find the evidence of this at the end of the first gospel of John which is actually her gospel. And Christ said, "If it is my will for her to remain until I come, of what concern is that to you?" Remember this Gnostic gospel has been edited. The son of MAN is within you. The Christ is within you. You are to become him

49

and he becomes you. You are to come into being, to become again an eternal light water soul. The way you were before this dead material universe came into being. You must do it while you are here, alive, and become the here and now. Know the truth. Become the truth and the truth shall set you free.

Here is how. Your mind has been divided in two with the most part connected with the Father and the least part connected with this dead world. Your soul has been divided from your spirit. Your goal is to get your soul back inside your spirit. Your soul is now on the outside of your spirit, together with the least part of your mind. You see, your soul and your outer mind are now together. Your Spirit is in the deepest part within you, and corruption cannot enter it. And your Father Mind or inner mind is between your spirit and your soul.

You are like this . You must become like this . Then you will become a Christ again. (Pattern=**Soul**, Black=**The Mother**, White=**The Father**)

You see, your soul is now male. It wants. You must make it again female. Female has. Your soul cannot enter the spirit with a polluted mind. It must become pure again to become female. You purify it by destroying the dead Aeons or by changing them back into living Aeons. This is the anointing. The best way to do this is to take them into yourself, and yourself being the inner Father mind. Remember he is perfect life and death cannot exist in life. So take your outer mind in to change your soul. Then you will be able to enter your spirit again. This is the true baptism. Your spirit is the inner water that your outer soul water must enter. There is a Gnostic saying, "There is water within water. There is light within light." Understand?

50

Become who you are and not who you are now not. Know thy self and become known. Know everything and everything will know you. Make the two in one. Become one and the same. Become a single one.

Before I end this chapter I will show you a picture of Christ where there is a cross behind his head. Remember that a cross is not a crucifix. At the top of and at the left and the right points of the cross there are three letters or symbols. In this point in time or era, there is a reason why English is a dominant language. This is the work of the Holy Spirit. Well these three letters are W, O, and N. These three letters spell out three different words of power. Two of the words have two powers each.

One of the words is NOW. Well, by now you should know this power and the meaning of this word.

Another of the words is WON. Remember the mind sees in images not spelling. So the two powers here are, won like one, meaning do your magic from the one or the Christ, The two in one. The other is WON as in victory that you have already WON.

The third word is OWN. The first power to this word is own like to do your magic from within by your OWN self. And the last power, this is to be who you are. Be your OWN self. Create your own values, your own ideas. Own your possessions, do not rent or owe but OWN.

If there is anything you do not understand, just go inside yourself for any answer. For every bit of knowledge of everything is there.

The Fifth Age
2012 December 21st the End of 7 the End of the World

December 21st 2012 ends the 4th material age and begins the 5th Age of Idea. The ideal age where now the idealists will reign bringing peace and harmony again to mankind. Ending the reign of the selfish, the takers, the materialists. This is the end of days and the beginning of the joyful lives of the Children of Light who are all the perfect day. This is not the end of the earth or of the humans on it. Remember I said that you must resurrect from while you are alive in a living body. But this is in fact the end of the world.

Know this, that the world is not the earth. The world and the earth are two completely different things. The earth is a planet where eternal living souls are living in human bodies. The world is the system of things, the way things are. But this is about to change. The world started 15 billion years ago. It is an order that god made. Why do you think god so loved the world? He made it.

This is the world, "I am god and I am above and greater than all." Next under him and above all the rest were the 11 other gods that the first god made. Then under them were the angels. After humans began living here on earth this continued with the kings who ruled over everyone, and under kings, generals and so on and so on. And this system of things continues to this day, with governments taking the place of the kings and religion taking the place of the gods.

At one time religion had more power when the kings were fading out and government was making its start. This time was terrible because religion was torturing, raping, and murdering many by the millions. You were commanded to be a so called Christian, or Muslim, or a Jew, and if you refused then you were burned alive. Thank goodness government eventually over powered religion. But even so we are still ruled by corruption.

So today the world is in fact, government, religion, and the secret societies that tell government what to do. Notice that all three of these corrupt entities have been and are still trying to keep women out. Remember as I said before, that anything that tries to make the female MAN less equal to the male MAN has to be evil.

I will explain further of the differences of the two kinds of ages and why it all has to do with Aeons.

You see, during a material age the dominant Aeons are the dead Aeons, because material is dead. During an ideal age then the eternal living Aeons are dominant for idea is eternal and comes from eternal mind and life.

Here is how the change comes. From an ideal to a material age, the change comes terrible and chaotic, like with a great earth covering flood. From a material to an ideal age it comes peaceful and serene.

You see, the planets, the suns, the solar systems, the galaxies, and in fact the whole universe is spinning all circular from and to negative and positive points. There are two great equal halves. While passing through the negative half, this is the power of the dead Aeons. While passing through the positive half this is the power of the living Aeons. Well the planets are about to line up and cross going now into the positive cycle or half. Also our galaxy is changing or crossing. This is called the Eight Spoked Wheel. Some call it the 13th Zodiac. But it is best to be understood as the Fifth Age, the age of the female MAN or the age of woman. This is the age of the five pointed star or the age of water or life or the Age of Aquarius.

And let me show you how this all comes and works together. It is with these numbers 0, 1, and 2. Look at the numbers here, 12/21/2012 and here, 120,000 years ago. And here, something god said in Genesis, since man is also flesh, I will cut his days short to 120 years. 12, 21,120, all 12, 12, 12. All the cycles and all the seasons are of 12.

Remember the System of 12? The gods once said (it is in the bible) that a day to them is like a thousand years. Well in the eternal realm there are 120 great children. They are the seed of Seth. 60 male and 60 female. And Adam and Eve came here exactly 120,000 years ago from the date December 21, 2012. So one of these great children comes at the end of a thousand year time period. The last child came at the end of the first thousand year and the first child will or has come at the end of the last thousand year. You may have heard the first shall come last and the last shall come first.

The governments and religion want you to be afraid of this great change. But it is because they are afraid. Their time is done. They speak of and they tell you to beware of a so called Anti-Christ. But they are the anti Christs. They are afraid of this one who will open the eyes of everyone, bringing freedom and oneness to all. We will be united again.

There is a song of which a young girl sings. A young girl called the artist Zeee. This song is called, "The Interpretation (of Imagine by John Lennon)." Search for this song and listen to the lyrics. She sings of how we once were united before god split our brains and how we will again be united in the Fifth Age.

Remember again how the gods said that a day to them is like a thousand years? Well this place of time and material is of theirs and we are called a perfect day, because where we come from there is no night. In fact there is not even time. So a perfect day is eternal. So with this in mind remember Christ said that he would return on the third day. Two thousand years ago from 12/21/2012 was when he returned to the eternal realm. And 12/21/2012 is the beginning of the third day, the third thousand year period. Well he also said look not to the clouds or the sky for my return. This is something that religion wants you to believe. He said but look for me within you for I am within you all. So on the third day he will return from within us all. This is when we will be aware of him that he is within us. And that he is us and that we are him. And we will all become Christs as he is Christ, for we are all equal and far greater than this whole pathetic material universe.

Know thy self. Know that you are true. Know that you are the truth that you are the perfect day and in you dwells the light of eternal continual success. Know that your will is the Father's will. Because you are the Father and the Father is you. You are the Mother and the Mother is you. Make the two in one and know that you are also the Son. When you are without corruption then you are perfect. So then when you are perfect then your will, will also be perfect. This is why it is your will be done, for your will, will always be good.

So then fear not and welcome to you the coming age, the Fifth Age of MAN.

More Knowledge
(Making More Sense)
The Holy War

A king named Constantine said he saw a crucifix and that the crucifix spoke to him with the voice of Jesus and said go conquer in my name. This is such bull because while Christ was walking the earth as Jesus he never ever said to kill or conquer. Well this king made up this lie as an excuse to start a so called holy war called the Crusades. And the three warring combatants in this war were the so called Christians, the Muslims, and the Jews. These are the three great religions of which all three worship the same dead god who was a murderer, a liar, and loved to watch humans conquering one another. And you see they worship him and do his will by killing each other. This makes no sense and no war could ever be holy.

The Knights Templar

Now I will tell you the mystery of the Knights Templar.

There were nine knights in France who were experienced warriors who had fought in the Crusades. These knights found out that the original scriptures of Christ or the Gnostic scriptures were in a secret place in Jerusalem. They got this information from the Cathar, the people who were taught the truth by Mary Magdalene. These hidden scriptures were the last known Gnostic scriptures. Well, after the Knights Templar found these scriptures and read through them, they had found out for themselves that everything that religion has been teaching was a lie. For these were the original scriptures of Christ.

Then the knights decided to do an evil thing, or a worldly thing. They black mailed the church by saying if the church didn't give them certain rights and pay them a multitude of money that they would expose the truth to all.

So the Church bought the scriptures from the Templars and locked them up in the Vatican Vaults. All other Gnostic scriptures were ordered to be burned that they were heresy. Also all people who knew about the truth or were in possession of these scriptures were put to death. They were usually burned alive. But the church did not count on that these same scriptures would come to us hundreds of years later, in 1945.

Near Nag Hammadi, Egypt these Gnostic scriptures were unearthed. They had been hidden in jars by some Gnostic Christians and buried there to be discovered almost 2,000 years later. The Holy Spirit caused this to happen that the Children of Light be able to read them passing into the Age of Knowledge, the Fifth Age.

After the Knights Templar did their deal with the church they then created credit and began to become extremely wealthy, so wealthy that the church and the king of France became in debt to them. So eventually the king and the church destroyed the Knights Templar instead of paying their debt to them.

The Knights Templar gave birth to the secret societies of today, or the societies with secrets. Notice that all so called secret societies, all governments, and all religions have much in common. This is because the heads of these three entities know of the truth, though they are not the truth. They hate the truth. You see, the heads of these entities are the only ones who know of it. The millions of their followers, however, do not know of the truth, and they are all misled.

Notice, I will say again that these three entities always keep women out. Female MAN is equal to male MAN. So when the female MAN is finally free and made to be completely equal here on earth everything will get fixed and goodness will ensue. Unity will come again and it's just around the corner.

The most popular and known about of these secret societies, are the so called Free Masons.

The Free Masons

The heads of the secret societies know of the truth but just like government and religion, won't share the truth. And all of these three promote the dead god belief.

Now the symbol that the masons use, the compass and the square, is representing two things: a six pointed star which is actually two triangles united or the female and the male united, and their symbol also represents two five pointed stars. But you must have a keen Coptic eye to see them. They also say that the G in their symbol stands for god. This is not true. The G stands for Gnosis.

You see they know of the truth yet they hide it. The Free Masons started the USA. And notice how a five pointed star represents each united state. If the five pointed star is evil then why do so many powerful entities use it?

Here is the Free Masons most sacred secret. They call themselves the "Free Masons." You know what free means. Here is what Masons means. It means they are the sons of MA; M meaning MAN or the Holy Spirit, and A meaning Adamas or Adam, which means Father. So then they are hiding the fact that they know of the truth and they are saying that they are the free sons of Christ that they know of the true trinity which is the Father the Mother and the Son yet they promote the dead god.

There is a Gnostic saying that goes, "blaspheme against the Father or the Son and thou shalt be forgiven, but blaspheme against the Mother and thou shalt not be forgiven neither on earth nor in heaven." Well, by knowing the truth which is the Holy Spirit and promoting the dead god is a major blaspheme against the Holy Spirit.

And all three entities do this. These three entities, government, religion, and the so called secret societies have been blaspheming against the Holy Spirit for just less than 2,000 years. Well, they are in big trouble.

Revelation Gospel

The last gospel in the New Testament is the most bogus gospel of all. Some religions try to say that this gospel came from the Apostle John, but the truth is that this gospel was written by some person of whom no one knows anything about what so ever, named John. And all we know of this John person is that he wrote this on an island called Patmos.

Well back in those days when there was not a cure for a disease and insanity, isolated places were set up for people with these incurable and contagious disorders. For example, there was a place called the Valley of the Lepers. This place was set up for damned people who had leprosy to live out the rest of their short lives. Well, the island of Patmos was a place for the crazy and insane.

So revelation was written by some crazy and insane person that we know nothing about. There were many other apocalyptic scriptures to choose from at that time to put into the bible, but religion picked this one since it is so ridiculous and makes no sense at all. Religion chose this one so that they could make up things and say things in it to mean whatever they wanted.

So forget about the gospel of revelation. It is irrelevant and makes no sense. Only the truth makes sense. Read from the truth.

The Number 7 god's Number

The number seven, all think that this is a lucky number. Well this was god's favorite number because of the seven-ness of the week.

The greatest number of all is the number that came because of the one who came forth first. This is the Holy Spirit and her number is five.

So know that five is far greater than seven. There is no power in seven there is only power in five. The power of the first five Aeons to come forth, and these I have explained earlier. So be with five and not with seven.

Homosexuality

So called homosexuality, some have said that this is a genetic disorder, but how could this be? Some bodies have come to be with many different disorders. I do not know all the answers to everything yet, but to know anything all one need do is go inside and all the answers are there.

Even if a body is born with both sexual organs, it will only have one soul. And in the most common cases like gay and lesbian, it is simple to know and to understand that a gay human male body has a female MAN soul within it and vice versa for the lesbian female body.

Now bisexuality can be explained for human women like this. You must know that we have all had many past lives and when a beautiful woman belonged to a harem, she was not allowed to have sex with any other man but her master or king or chieftain. And when masters had so many women in their harem, they could not satisfy them all being so greedy for lust. So then the women would find pleasure and satisfaction with each other.

Simply put, we are not our bodies we are our souls. So to know another person is to know who they are. It is to know their soul and do not judge someone by their body.

True Magic and Black Magic

True magic can only come from the here and now, from the power of Christ. There is no such thing as black magic or evil magic. For things from death or material have no creative power of life in them to engender anything. So when it seems that black magic is working on someone it is only because that someone or the victim believes in the black magic. Therefore it is safe to say that this believer in this black magic is his own self-curser. It is his own belief that destroys him.

So believe not in false things that cannot come about by dead powers. In fact, there is no need to believe at all, but know. Know thy self. Know the truth.

Symbols and Symbolism

Many times when people have prayed they ask Christ or Jesus to give them a sign, but in the Gnostic scriptures or the scriptures of knowledge, Christ asks to give him a sign. There is also a Gnostic scripture that says, "The kingdom of heaven is spread out throughout the earth but people do not see it." Well I can tell you this, that I can see it everywhere, every day.

A logo is a symbol or a sign. A trademark is a sign or is a trinity MAN symbol. These are all signs or sign posts to represent values that do good for mankind, so then when a business uses a sign to represent their business (that is a trinity MAN sign), then their business will flourish and they will be extremely successful. But if a business or any entity uses trinity MAN symbols and are doing corruption, then they will eventually pay for their blasphemy to the Holy Spirit in a big way.

The greatest and most obvious sign ever used to give eternal power of truth to a business was the first Chrysler symbol, the sign for the Chrysler automobile. Ever notice the way Chrysler sounds? The sign they used was a five pointed star with a pentacle circling the star.

This same symbol was carved in a cave wall in France by the Cathar. The Inquisition discovered it looking for treasure.

Little did they know that the knowledge of this symbol is the treasure. After the church first saw this symbol they immediately made the five pointed star out to be evil.

When you go out for a drive look all around you and you will see the many different trinity MAN symbols that are created as a sign to the true Christ to give their business true power or the power of truth. And only the founders of the businesses who know of this truth are ever successful. With only the knowledge of this truth can your business be successful.

I will show you many signs to look for. And depending on the different mixtures of these signs, they are all speaking different words of imagery and they are all speaking the same thing. You see the mind sees in images and/or signs. The inner mind sees this because the outer mind is blind. But when the outer mind becomes aware of this, then that mind becomes more powerful and becomes closer and more in unity with the inner mind.

Here we go. Look for three rectangles. This means of course the three meaning the trinity, and also being rectangles is the 3×4points=12 points, which means the power of the eternal 12 Aeons of the first created perfect MAN. Notice that most governments use this on their national flags ▬.They use this with three different colors.

Now here are many TM symbols to look for ○ ☆ +×
⊗ ⊕ Z N A V W M C H △⅄ ℗ .

Also look for two images that mirror each other 🦎🦎 . A hand with two fingers together means make the two in one.

Here are some examples of some existing symbols.

Look for the treasure and you will see it. Create your own symbol to Christ. Do your own business. Be who you are, and not what the world wants you to be. Remember that the Holy Spirit works through us all. So some of these businesses had the first person, who knew of this, the person who was the inventor, and this person set up his sign. But many of these businesses put up a trinity MAN sign and don't even know what they have done. It is because the Holy Spirit is working through them to bring out this product or commodity to the people on the earth. If we all did our own business, if we all worked with each other instead of for each other, we would all be rich and happy. This day is upon us. Soon we will all be united and free again.

How to Destroy the World That Did Bind You

They say the world will end and it will. Not the earth or the people on it but the system of things will end. The way things have been. The world.

Well, remember that I told you that there is a black hole in the center of every galaxy that is drawing in and consuming the material bringing it back to the eternal realm? Well like the center of the galaxies, you are a black hole. The black hole in the galaxy consumes material and the black hole in you consumes the dead world Aeons of material. The black hole within you is the Father, your inner mind, your knowing self, your awareness.

Well the Gnostics and the Cathar who were also called the perfect knew that to become perfect is to perfect the outer mind by bringing the dead Aeons that pollute it, in, into your inner mind, into your awareness.

The action in this perfection is done in motion and rest, motion meaning E-motion or energies in motion. Energies in motion come from thoughts and dead thoughts come because of dead Aeons. If we only thought good thoughts then all of our energies in motion would be good and we would only create good circumstance. But bad circumstance comes settling as dead world feelings which are dead world emotions. These dead world emotions give the dead Aeons more power to keep us down, to keep us in failure, to keep us unhappy, to kill us.

The first Gnostic Christians, the Apostles, called this the left and the right. Know that the dead Aeons were placed on the left hand side of the brain and the eternal living Aeons were placed on the right hand side. Notice left and right hand side. Therefore, your left side of your body is governed by the right side of your brain. So the left side of your brain is actually the right hand side and the right side of your brain is the left hand side.

Christ says, "Take up your cross." This doesn't mean lift up a crucifix and suffer, this means to, with your two fingers cross your forehead from right to left taking the death to the life, and then crossing up from your chin past your forehead to lift you up.

The Catholics know of this and all their misled followers diminish themselves by going the wrong way. They are giving themselves more death. You could say that they are giving themselves the sign of the crucifix and not the sign of the true cross.

By making the sign of the cross in the right way, taking up your cross, you are making a conviction to your inner mind that you know what you are doing and in your thinking as knowledge you are taking the dead left to the living right in turn you are taking the outer mind into the inner mind.

Know that each dead Aeon can only be taken to its original root. So take hate to love, take poverty to wealth, take want to have, and so on and so on. There are many different ways to do this. And when you finally resolve all of the dead Aeons back into their roots from which they came then you will become perfect. When you have become perfect then it is time to make the two in one which is the joining of the Father and the Mother of whom will now clothe you once again with indestructible eternal life. This is when you become a Christ.

Remember our first super hero, Superman? Well Superman is actually a representation of a Christ. He cannot be destroyed. He is eternal. His material body cannot be harmed. He does not lie. He can fly. He can do anything. And look at his trinity MAN symbol. It is an S meaning the Father who is super or the supreme, being surrounded by a five pointed symbol or pentacle, super being Father and Man being Mother. Super MAN being Christ, the Son.

Here is one way to release yourself from the dead Aeons, how to destroy the dead energies in motion, to destroy dead feelings. Remember that your awareness is the Father within you. So bring up into your awareness dead emotions, dead feelings, and dead Aeons. These all three are the same thing.

Relax and think of your greatest fear, the thing you fear the most. Relax and draw this fear up into your awareness and allow all of the sensations and bad feelings associated with this fear to be. Resist them not. Allow them to be here. Now welcome them in. Allow yourself or the Father within you to rest into them. Relax and continue to think of things that hinder you, bad moments you remember, bad things that happen to you, and people that piss you off and give you a hard time, and continue to relax and just welcome all of this death into your awareness. And give thanks to yourself, who is the Father within you, in knowing that you are consuming the dead Aeons of the world.

There will be moments as you keep doing this when you will consume or destroy death that has been holding you down for a long time. When this happens you may burst out laughing hysterically. This is normal. You are experiencing the joy of becoming free. Know that death cannot live in life. Be aware of it and welcome it in. This is one way of doing this. "It is in motion and in rest."

Use the Rest of the Father to consume the dead energies that were set in motion. Go inside yourself. Ask from within what to do and how to do it. Find new and other ways to free yourself until you become perfect. Then you can truly become a "Superman" or a Christ.

Conclusion

In conclusion, I will now show you the mystery and the knowledge of the "Lord's Prayer" or "the Our Father." Like I said before this is a Gnostic prayer but people do not know. Christ said to his Apostles, "Do not go to the synagogue or church to pray." You see Christ never cared for churches because they go with religion. And Christ is opposed to religion. He said, "For those who go to the synagogue to pray do not receive the thing of which they pray for." But instead they receive the thing that they are really caring about. And that is to be seen of men. To be seen that they are doing good. This is what they are really concerned with because they don't really believe in prayer. He said, "Go into a room by yourself where there is no one else and pray to the Father that is within you. Then you will receive your reward of which you pray for." Then the disciples said, "How then do we pray to the Father?" and the lord said, "Like this." Christ then recites the Lord's Prayer to them for the first time.

This is the greatest magical prayer of all, but people don't know its power or what it means or even how to use it. They just blindly say the prayer. Here is the hidden magic of the Lord's Prayer. First of all you must know that the kingdom of heaven is your inner mind. So then, "My father who art in heaven," this obviously is saying that the Father is in heaven, heaven being our inner mind. "Hallowed be thy name." This means that the Father's name is Holy being that this is the only name that he can be called since he has no name. Now pay attention here, "Thy kingdom come thy will be done." By saying this you are calling the inner mind forth (thy kingdom come). Now remember that your will is the Father's will. So when you

67

say, "Thy will be done." You are saying that whatever you have willed to be, will be. Now listen to this, "On earth as it is in heaven." So that which you imaged and willed in your mind is to now be manifested here on earth. It is to now be here on earth as you have imaged it in your mind's eye. And the rest is, "give me this day my daily bread." Remember that we are a perfect day coming from the eternal realm time is not in us though we are here and now trapped in it, we are still a perfect day. So you are saying to give to individually you (this day) "give me this day my daily bread." And bread is a Gnostic Coptic term meaning knowledge, "daily" meaning you are here in time and "bread" meaning give me the knowledge I need being here from day to day. "And forgive me my trespasses as I forgive those who trespass against me." This means that you will only be forgiven if you also forgive. But what it means most of all is that by forgiving someone of the evil that they have put out that you have allowed them to put upon you will now be released and you won't have to hold on to that corruption anymore. And the final part, "And lead me not into temptation but deliver me from evil." This part has been edited by religion. It has been changed. The inner mind will not comprehend, not. So you are really hearing, lead me into temptation. And the very last part is even worse being that the last word you say and hear is, evil. Instead the last part could go like this, "and lead me into wisdom and knowledge and deliver me into the eternal goodness of truth."

You may have also noticed that I have explained this magical Gnostic prayer as I am speaking it alone and by myself using words like "my father" and "give me my" as opposed to "our father" and "give us our." The reason why I do this is because religion changed it so that many could say it in a church. But it will have no power saying it as a group. Remember Christ said not to go to church but to say this prayer alone by yourself.

Why then would you say this prayer by using the word we? Understand? Learn this power. Know this power and use it.

I have a saying that if it doesn't make sense (cents) than it is probably making dollars, but not for you.

I have looked outside for some of the explanations I have found but this is only because my inside told me where to look. I first always go inside. Inside you is the truth. Inside you is the kingdom of heaven. Learn to go inside for all of the answers. Your innerness will sometimes tell you from within and sometimes your innerness will guide you and show you where to look outside. But if you look outside for the answers, deceit is always ready to lie to you and steer you the wrong way. Know that you are not your body that you are not of this world that this whole material universe is beneath you, that you are far greater than this world could never imagine. Know thy self and be known by self. Know everything and everything will know you. Back your magical eternal powers up with the Amen. Know that you are Christ and Christ is you, that your mind is a part of all mind, that your spirit is a part of all spirit, that your unique individual, original soul belongs to eternal life, and that it can never die, that you are here and now but that you will eventually be only NOW, without this crappy here. Become who you now know you are! Be the super MAN that you are meant to be.

I am fearless for you my brothers and sisters. For I love you
all.
Seek the Christ within you so that your inner eye and inner
ear be opened,
for he is waiting for you to open the door.

69

CPSIA information can be obtained at www.ICGtesting.com
Printed in the USA
LVOW10s1818150415

434687LV00028B/23/P